WIL'S BONES

Discussion Guide

A TOOL FOR
CHRISTIAN READING GROUPS

Engage Publishing
Port Townsend, Washington

ENGAGE
PUBLISHING

Published by Engage Publishing
P.O. Box 1452, Port Townsend, WA 98368
www.engagepublishing.com

07 06 05 04 03 — 5 4 3 2 1

PUBLISHER'S CATALOGING-IN-PUBLICATION DATA

Wil's bones discussion guide : a tool for Christian reading groups.
-- Port Townsend, WA : Engage Publishing, 2003.

p. ; cm.

Sold in sets of 6 copies each.
ISBN: 1-930892-13-6

1. Bowen, Kevin. Wil's bones. 2. Christian fiction--History and criticism. I. Engage Publishing. II. Title. III. Wil's bones.

PS3602.O946 W557 2003
813.6--dc21 0308

Printed in the United States of America

Contents

WIL'S BONES

Discussion Guide

Therefore, I urge you, brothers, in view of God's mercy, to offer your bodies as living sacrifices, holy and pleasing to God—this is your spiritual act of worship. Do not conform any longer to the pattern of this world, but be transformed by the renewing of your mind. Then you will be able to test and approve what God's will is—his good, pleasing and perfect will. For by the grace given me I say to every one of you: Do not think of yourself more highly than you ought, but rather think of yourself with sober judgment, in accordance with the measure of faith God has given you.

Romans 12:1–3

Introduction

It is somewhat unusual to have a discussion guide for a work of fiction. *Wil's Bones,* however, was written for more than entertainment purposes. It was also written with the hope of challenging readers to confront an issue that is much more important than a few brief hours of reading.

The goal of this discussion guide is not to turn anyone into an expert on *Wil's Bones*. Instead, it uses *Wil's Bones* to facilitate reflection and thought on, among other things, the biggest issue in history—Christ's resurrection.

Chapter 1 addresses the story, plots, and characters in *Wil's Bones*. Chapters 2 and 3 focus on two aspects of the resurrection of Jesus Christ—the historical reality of Jesus' resurrection and the absolute centrality of Christ's resurrection to Christian faith. Chapter 4 looks at the sayings that precede some chapters as well as a few comments by characters in *Wil's Bones*. Chapter 5 deals with the application of some of the issues addressed in this guide and, hopefully, in your group's discussion and reflection.

You will note that there are spaces after each question and some blank lines at the end of each chapter. Though we hope this guide will be used to stimulate discussion (not a lot of writing and busy work) we also believe that such discussion might be richer if each person has an opportunity to record insights, either one's own or those that come up during conversation. These blank areas provide a handy place to jot down such insights.

Clearly it would be most beneficial if every member of the group read *Wil's Bones* prior to the discussion or working through this guide. And, though it might be possible to cover the whole book in one or two meetings, it is highly likely you will want to spend more time than that. A total of five meetings would be ideal.

The following are some suggestions as to how to use this booklet.

Suggestion 1:
Decide how much time you want to spend going through the discussion guide. Because there are five chapters, divide your allotted time into five equal sessions. Next, select a facilitator (for each session or for all five). Finally, cover one chapter per session, with the facilitator reading a question and then letting the discussion occur in an open forum format or with everyone taking a turn.

It is important that the facilitator keep the conversation focused on the question (and the chapter) and keep the conversation moving in order to cover the chapter in the allotted time.

Suggestion 2 (recommended):
This option is similar to Suggestion 1 except that, prior to each session, group members individually complete the section of the discussion guide that will be addressed. One

advantage of this approach is that it helps to keep the discussion on track.

Suggestion 3:
This option might be considered if the reading group is large or if you desire more intimate discussions. Under this scenario, the group breaks into smaller groups, or cells. Each cell discusses a chapter (or a group of questions within a chapter), and then the entire group gathers again to summarize.

It is Engage Publishing's sincerest desire that this discussion guide will be a catalyst for constructive thought and discussion, and that those who work their way through the guide will be changed.

In Christ and for His glory,
Engage Publishing

With many similar parables Jesus spoke the word to them, as much as they could understand. He did not say anything to them without using a parable. But when he was alone with his own disciples, he explained everything.

Mark 4:33–34

Chapter 1 The Book

Wil's Bones was written for both Christians and non-Christians. This discussion guide is directed specifically to Christians.

The author's primary purpose for writing *Wil's Bones* was evangelistic. He wanted to present the message of Christ in a way that would allow people who otherwise would not listen to the gospel to encounter it. Aware that mystery/suspense thrillers appeal to many people, he decided to write a novel that incorporated Christian theological material in the plot, similar to the way John Grisham uses legal issues or Tom Clancy uses military information.

His first challenge, though, was to make Christian plot material interesting to those who usually don't want to have anything to do with Christianity.

The author concluded that the destruction of Christianity could possibly be of interest to non-Christians and decided to use this as his theme (remembering that it is only fiction). He knew that, in order to destroy Christianity, Christianity would have to be defined. His intention was to present the gospel as part of that definition.

Why do you think the author chose the resurrection for his plot material?

Was his choice of the resurrection the best choice? (What else, if anything, would destroy Christianity?)

The author chose Christ's resurrection because nothing else is more central to our faith. He knew that if someone could prove Christ's resurrection didn't happen, it would drive a stake through the heart of Christianity.

What reasons did Wil have to want to kill Christianity?

Do you know anyone like Wil or Wil's dad?

Wil's dad had a significant impact on Wil's spiritual formation and his hatred of Christianity.

? *How do the faith and actions of other people, particularly those who call themselves Christians, affect others?*

? *Can you think of anyone who has been driven away from Christ by the actions of those who call themselves Christians?*

Wil's motive was developed in his upbringing, but it wasn't until he encountered a guest lecturer in college that he discovered a means to bring down his father's religion (p. 41–48).

? *What is your opinion of Keith McDonald's statements?*

? *Were his statements true? Explain.*

Now that Wil had his motive and his plan, he just needed the opportunity. Enter Kathreen Steele, the Israeli secret police, and the search for explosives at archaeological sites on which Wil was the pre-eminent expert.

? *How did you feel when they discovered the bones in the tomb?*

? *How did you feel when certain characters, and the world as a whole, began to believe that the discovered bones were, in fact, the bones of Jesus?*

? *When did you figure out they weren't the bones of Jesus? (No fair saying that you knew from the beginning because* Wil's Bones *is a Christian book!)*

One of the problems the author had with the plot was making the discovery of the bones convincing while also providing an "out."

? *What were some loopholes he left himself? (One hint can be found in John 19:33.)*

? *Why was it important that none of Jesus' bones were broken? (Hint: Exodus 12:46, Numbers 9:12.)*

? *What did you think of Pastor Wally's comments on the broken bones passage (p. 113)?*

The author used a number of stereotypes to communicate the theological points he was trying to make. The panel members on the "Royal Lawrence Show" in Chapter 23 are examples of such stereotypes.

? *Define and discuss the different perspectives of the panel members. Was the portrayal of the three non-Christian perspectives fair to people who hold such positions?*

? *Do you know anyone like those three characters on the panel with Steve? Describe them.*

In addition to Steve Halterman and Keith McDonald, what other voices presented Christ in other parts of the book?

If you are familiar with Bunyan's *Pilgrim's Progress*, you are likely familiar with the literary technique of giving a character a name to match the character's role or traits. For instance, Christian, the main character in *Pilgrim's Progress,* is obviously intended to represent Christians. The character who represents the atheist perspective is named Atheist. The character who represents despair is named Giant Despair, etc.

In Wil's Bones*, two characters' names are intended to be representative of kinds of people. Who are they? (If you can't figure it out, send an e-mail to Whoarethey@engagepublishing.com. We will get back to you.)*

How do their personalities or roles match their names? Give some examples.

Does your life represent what it means to be a Christian?

Although Wil was very willful and driven, he also had integrity. Wil's integrity becomes important to the story's development near the end of the book.

? *Discuss Wil's integrity and how it affected the plot.*

? *A few other characters in the book were intended to be takeoffs of actual people. Who was each of these characters based on?*

- *Keith McDonald*

- *Royal Lawrence*

- *Kenny Reno*

Too frequently, when Christians are portrayed in contemporary novels or movies, the portrayal is unfair and unrealistic. Often the characters who are intended to represent Christians convey hypocrisy, New Age ideas, and/or heresy. In *Wil's Bones*, Steve Halterman is intended to be the example of a true Christian.

? *Was he a good example of a true Christian?*

Discuss why you think he was or was not a believable character.

Was his theology correct? Explain.

One criticism of the book by some Christian readers was that Wil and Hope, even though they were not Christians, should not have lived together because sex outside of marriage is wrong. Other criticisms centered on the presence of alcohol, Wil's disrespect for authority, and the use of the term "bimbo." According to these Christian readers, such material should not be in a Christian book. A few Christians were so upset by the book's content they sent unkind notes to the author. Some Christian store owners were so bothered by the book's content that they refused to carry *Wil's Bones* in their stores.

Was the author encouraging sin (sex outside of marriage, drunkenness, etc.)?

Was the author's portrayal of Wil and Hope's relationship indecent?

? *Is it wrong for a Christian author to include such material in a story? Can you think of reasons it is appropriate to include such material?*

? *Does the Bible include such material? Why?*

The following are a few general questions for discussion.

? *Who was your favorite character?*

? *What was your favorite part of the book?*

? *Is it possible to train a cat the way Wil had trained Napoleon?*

? *Do you think* Wil's Bones *presents the gospel?*

In *Wil's Bones*, significant attention was given to relationships. Perhaps the most compelling was the relationship between Steve and Wil.

? *Describe Steve's relationship with Wil.*

At a book-signing event in Texas, the author was encouraging a Christian sister to use *Wil's Bones* as a tool with non-Christian friends. The woman countered, proudly, that she did not have any non-Christian friends. The author reminded her that Jesus frequently spent time with the ungodly. He also suggested that salt that stays in a saltshaker is no good to anyone.

? *Do you have any relationships similar to that of Steve and Wil? Why or why not?*

? *Do you know any non-Christians who might like* Wil's Bones?

Chapter notes

And if Christ has not been raised, our preaching is useless and so is your faith. More than that, we are then found to be false witnesses about God, for we have testified about God that he raised Christ from the dead. But he did not raise him if in fact the dead are not raised. For if the dead are not raised, then Christ has not been raised either. And if Christ has not been raised, your faith is futile; you are still in your sins. Then those also who have fallen asleep in Christ are lost. If only for this life we have hope in Christ, we are to be pitied more than all men. But Christ has indeed been raised from the dead, the firstfruits of those who have fallen asleep.

1 Corinthians 15:14–20

Chapter 2
The Historical Resurrection

One of the many exciting things that resulted from *Wil's Bones* is that it has led to incredible opportunities for the author to speak to non-Christians about Christ and His resurrection. Because the plot hinges on Christ's resurrection (and the nonexistence of Jesus' bones) the author has been able to discuss Christ's resurrection in secular bookstores, on a New Age radio program, in public schools, and on secular television. The author has also had the opportunity to talk to many people who call themselves Christians but who have abandoned the historical Jesus and embraced everything from ancient heresies to modern myths concerning Jesus.

In various forums and conversations, the author of *Wil's Bones* has heard non-Christians state a number of amazing, and frankly bizarre, beliefs concerning Jesus—everything from "Jesus never existed" to "Jesus was an alien." Some theories were incredibly elaborate. Some of them were outright lunacy. Most of them didn't have a shred of historical evidence to back them up. And, none of them could hold a candle to the overwhelming arguments and evidence supporting the historical reality of Christ's resurrection.

What is the evidence for the resurrection of Christ? (Hint: historical, circumstantial, eyewitness, changed lives.)

What are some of the ideas and false teachings you have heard about the resurrection?

Why do you think people want to believe wild theories as opposed to the actual evidence?

What disturbed the author more than the unsupported opinions about the resurrection voiced by non-Christians were the comments he heard from some sincere and well-meaning Christians.

During a signing at a bookstore in Arizona, a woman introduced herself to the author as a Christian. When the author explained that his book was about an archaeologist who claimed to have found the bones of Jesus, the woman cut him off and joyously exclaimed, "Praise God! That's like finding Noah's ark!" The author kindly pointed out her error.

Explain why finding Noah's ark would be good and why finding Jesus' bones would be devastating.

The author has also been told (by Christians and non-Christians) that finding Jesus' bones would not be that big a deal. They claim that, even if Jesus did rise from the grave (like Lazarus in John 11), He merely died again, leaving behind his body (and bones).

Why is this idea not true? (See Acts: 1:9–11)

Still, let's suppose that the above theory is correct, that Jesus rose from the grave only to die again and leave behind His dead body.

What happened to the body?

By their teachings, the followers of Jesus were disrupting social order and threatening the authority and reputation of the Jewish and Roman leadership.

? *How unlikely do you think it is, if there was a body, that someone wouldn't have found and exposed the body in order to silence the followers of Jesus? Explain.*

Some Christians also said that finding the bones would not be that big a deal because Jesus' resurrection was only spiritual, not physical. In addition, many sincere Christians believe that if someone really did find the bones of Jesus, it wouldn't matter because they "have a spiritual relationship with Jesus."

? *What is wrong with the above ideas? (Comment: there are many things wrong with them, but one of them is found in Luke 24:1–7.)*

Wil's Bones makes the point that if someone did find Jesus' bones, then Jesus was not the Son of God as He claimed to be. If that were true, then having a relationship with Jesus would mean having a relationship with a dead liar or, at best, a well-intentioned lunatic who had rotted in the grave. The Bible is very clear that Jesus' resurrection was a physical as well as a spiritual event.

In addition, *Wil's Bones* makes the point that the testimony (unto death) of early Christians is evidence of the resurrection. It is important, however, to be careful with this piece of evidence.

Does dying for something you believe in make it true? Explain.

What makes a person's testimony true?

The fact is, many people have died for many different beliefs. That does not make their beliefs true. One thing that makes the early Christians' testimonies unique, particularly that of the disciples, is that they were eyewitnesses. The disciples did not die for a sincere belief they had learned from someone else. They died because they were eyewitnesses to Christ's resurrection. They could not deny that which they knew was true. Not one of the disciples recanted. This would be fairly compelling testimony in any court of law.

Can you imaging a situation in which 11 people would be willing to be tortured, crucified, beaten, exiled, or killed for what they all knew to be a fabrication they personally had concocted? Would you be willing to die for a religion you made up?

Those who claim the disciples concocted Christ's resurrection tend to ignore how stupid the disciples would have been to make up such a religion. Remember, the belief in Jesus' resurrection did not start until *after* many people had watched Jesus be humiliated, beaten, killed, and then placed in a tomb under Roman guard. Certainly, if the disciples wanted to fabricate a religion, they would have come up with something harder to disprove.

Keep in mind that for a group of fishermen and outcasts to steal and hide the body of a famous criminal under Roman guard would be no small task. If the disciples had been like the founders of other world religions, they would have claimed something that could not be factually refuted. For example, if they had claimed Jesus' resurrection was only spiritual, there would be no way to disprove it. As it was, they claimed that He rose from the grave and many people saw him. All their adversaries had to do was produce the body or find someone to confess that the whole thing was a hoax. They couldn't.

Can you think of any other religion or belief system that is based on something as objective and historical as the resurrection of Jesus?

It is important to know as many facts about the resurrection as possible. Praise God that, in His mercy, He has given us solid evidence of the truth of Christ's resurrection.

? *Why do you think so many Christians have forgotten about, or just not given enough thought to, the importance of the resurrection of Jesus?*

? *Discuss what you now know regarding the evidence of Christ's resurrection.*

? *Does it make sense that someone could call himself or herself a Christian and not know about the reality and historicity of Christ's resurrection? Explain.*

? *What is required to be a Christian (Romans 10:9)?*

The importance of the resurrection cannot be overstated, and knowing the facts of this crucial and actual event in history should be basic for all Christians. To that end, it is highly recommended that you consider studying more about it. Ask your pastor or priest about a good resource. The following also contain excellent information on the facts and historicity of Christ's resurrection.

The Third Day by Hank Hanegraaff
More Than A Carpenter by Josh McDowell
A Case for Christ by Lee Stroble
Mere Christianity by C.S. Lewis

? *Can you think of any other resources to suggest to the group? What are they?*

? *Are you prepared to share the truth, and defend the truth, of the most important event in history?*

Chapter notes

Now, brothers, I want to remind you of the gospel I preached to you, which you received and on which you have taken your stand. By this gospel you are saved, if you hold firmly to the word I preached to you. Otherwise, you have believed in vain. For what I received I passed on to you as of first importance: that Christ died for our sins according to the Scriptures, that he was buried, that he was raised on the third day according to the scriptures, and appeared to Peter, and then to the Twelve.

1 Corinthians 15:1–5

CHAPTER 3
The Centrality of the Resurrection

Read 1 Corinthians 15:1–20.

There is, perhaps, no other event in human history as important as the resurrection of Jesus. Yet, Christ's resurrection is much more than just a historical event. In it, Christians throughout history have found hope for the present and future.

On the wall of the author's home is a picture with an image of the Colosseum in Rome. The emperor sits in the place of honor. The crowd is clearly cheering for the lions that have encircled five Christians huddled in the center of the arena, about to be ripped to shreds. An elderly man in the middle stands tall with his hands raised to heaven, his eyes fixed on what is beyond the coming moment. A little child clings to his mother's neck. She can only reassure him that it will be all right. A young man and another woman wait, knowing they will soon be with the saints who have gone before them. Underneath the image are the words: "Faithful unto death."

The people in the picture represent the thousands of early believers who acknowledged Christ as the risen Lord, and died for it.

Do you think people like those in the picture would have died for Christ if He had not risen from the grave as He said He would to prove His claim to be God incarnate? Explain.

What would have happened to the disciples and Jesus' other followers if He hadn't risen? What message would they have spread and would it have changed so many lives?

If Christ had not risen, would we have even heard of Jesus?

Today Christians in China, Sudan, Pakistan, Indonesia, Columbia, North Korea, and other countries around the globe routinely stand before torturers and judges and "lions" because they name Jesus as their Lord. Many are killed because they will not recant their belief that Jesus is the Christ who rose from the grave.

These Christians stand firm in their hope of salvation, not because of a belief regarding the gifts of the Holy Spirit, not because of their convictions regarding the correct form of baptism, and not based on a doctrine of the last days. No, they remain faithful unto death because they know the Lord they serve has risen from the dead and that He has conquered death and made it possible for them to be reconciled to the Father for all eternity. It is the resurrection of Jesus that has been the basis of hope for Christians throughout history.

? *What gives Christians in America hope? (Yes, this is a judgmental question.)*

? *Where do you put* your *hope? Explain.*

? *How important is Christ's resurrection in your life?*

? *Would anyone else know Christ's resurrection is important to you? How?*

Those who have accepted God's gracious gift of eternal life through Christ Jesus will be resurrected after death. Because of Christ's resurrection, death cannot hold us. Instead, when our time on this earth ends, we will rise and spend all eternity in the presence and wonder and majesty and splendor and blessing and glory of our loving God.

? *Since this life is but a moment—a speck in time—why do Christians become so concerned about this life and neglect the more important, more eternal things, such as the salvation of those around us?*

According to the author, the most emotional chapter for him to write was Chapter 20, where Pastor Wally talks to his congregation. The author envisioned himself in the audience, looking to Pastor Wally as the last hope that perhaps the bones Wil had discovered were not the bones of Jesus. And then, Wally says they are!

? *What was your response when Pastor Wally tried to encourage the defeated congregation by saying, "Just because Jesus was not who He said He was does not mean there isn't much we can learn from His teachings," and "Besides, we are a family and we have much to offer each other"?*

How would you respond if you were somehow truly convinced Jesus had not risen?

At the end of the book Steve asks Wil, "What if Jesus really did rise from the dead and if He really was who He said He was?" (p. 243). This question was intended not only for Wil but also for the readers. The author wanted both Christians and non-Christians to really think that question through.

The fact is that God graciously provided a historical anchor to our faith with Christ's resurrection from the grave.

What is the appropriate response to this gracious act by God?

We Christians know Jesus did rise. Isn't it reasonable to assume that our knowledge of Christ's resurrection should affect our lives?

Has it affected your life? Did it matter to you today? How?

As we approach the last days of our lives, or of this era, we Christians should be focused on what really matters.

? *Since we say that our hope is based on Christ's resurrection, does it make sense that we spend so little time talking about it and so much time focused on other less important things?*

? *What would happen if we Christians spent more time talking with each other about Christ's resurrection and what it means for us?*

? *What would happen if we Christians spent more time talking to non-Christians about His resurrection?*

? *Who needs to hear from YOU?*

Chapter notes

"What do you think ... ?"

Matthew 17:25
Matthew 18:12
Matthew 22:42

Chapter 4
Sayings and Quotations

Have you ever been part of a lively debate about what a movie character meant when he said something out of the ordinary? Or have you ever (perhaps in an English class) wrestled with something someone wrote (perhaps Shakespeare or a poet your teacher made you read) and actually enjoyed the conversation and reflection?

Have you ever wondered why people are so fascinated with quotations that there are books of quotations, calendars of famous quotations, Web sites of quotable quotes, etc.?

? *Do you have a favorite quotation (not from* Wil's Bones*)?*

? *Why is it meaningful to you?*

The author of *Wil's Bones* wanted to take advantage of this penchant for sayings in order to present some ideas that would not have sounded right coming from one of the characters. The sayings preceding some chapters allowed him to address issues and ideas that touched on a theme of the book. He also hoped the sayings would stimulate readers' thoughts so that they might be more receptive to the book's message.

? *Was there one saying you liked more than any other? Why?*

? *Was there a saying you didn't like? Explain.*

? *Were any of the sayings theologically inconsistent with sound Christian doctrine?*

Truth is a big issue in *Wil's Bones*. Though the primary truth the author wanted people to focus on was the truth of Christ's resurrection, he also wanted people to think about truth in general.

On pages 54, 80, and 88 three successive sayings talk about truth. What is their combined message?

How does the question on page 110 tie into the chapter that follows (and the main issue of the book)?

But truth, we are so often told by today's cultural relativists, is in the mind of the individual. As Christians, we know that this is sheer hogwash. Truth is truth regardless of one's beliefs or perspective. Furthermore, though relativists tout open-mindedness, what they often mean is that everything is okay except Christianity. They cannot and will not accept the absolute truth revealed in Christ Jesus. On page 94, the author addresses this.

Discuss the saying on page 94. Is it true? Give some examples.

At the bottom of page 192 and the top of page 193 some comments are made about Wil's mistake that led to the fiasco he created. These comments tie into the sayings on pages 148 and 180. All three of these deal with bias and the loss of objectivity.

? *Read the above selections and discuss how bias can affect objectivity.*

? *Does having an opinion mean you cannot be objective? Explain.*

Another lie we often hear repeated is, "Ignorance is bliss." The people who say this usually mean it is better not to know about bad things. Let's look at this. If you are ignorant that a truck is going to run over you, how is it better to not know about it than to know and get out of the way? Those who argue that ignorance is bliss would say, if you couldn't get out of the way, then not knowing would be better. That is a matter of opinion. In any case, few things in life are that certain.

? *What does the saying on page 158 mean? Is it true?*

What does the saying on page 158 mean when applied to those who are ignorant of the gospel or the truth of the resurrection of Christ?

Two examples of integrity stand out in the book: Wil's decision to make sure the truth is known (that the bones were *not* Jesus' bones) even when it meant resuscitating the very thing he intensely wanted to destroy; and Steve's willingness to accept the truth (that they were the bones of Jesus) even if it meant absolute hopelessness to him (page 141).

What do you think the saying on page 202 means?

In the Epilogue the author tried to present the issue of the love of God the Father, demonstrated when Christ died on the cross. He hoped that, by tying it into the chapter's theme of fathers (Wil's becoming a father, Steve's loss of his son, and the father of the thief who died on the cross) non-Christians would hear, in a non-threatening way, about the amazing love of God.

? *What are some of your thoughts about Steve's comments to Wil and Hope in the Epilogue (starting at the bottom of page 241)?*

? *On page 236 there is a statement about parenthood. For those of you who are parents, is the statement on page 236 true? Explain.*

? *How would this statement apply to God the Father as He watched His Son Jesus die on the cross?*

Though the preceding are important issues, clearly the most important issue in *Wil's Bones* is the truth and centrality of Christ's resurrection. But, like many important things, the resurrection is frequently neglected and taken for granted.

A Christian woman who had read *Wil's Bones* told the author that, prior to reading *Wil's Bones*, she had not thought much about Christ's resurrection. Then, while reading his book, she began to consider how she would feel if the resurrection had not happened. She said that such thoughts brought back dark memories in her life, and a sense of hopelessness. After reading *Wil's Bones,* she had a new appreciation for the hope found in Christ's resurrection.

The author hopes that Christians who read *Wil's Bones* will be encouraged to refocus on the resurrection rather than the many other issues that seem to preoccupy and divide us. To that end, he inserted the question on page 116.

? *What is the answer to the question on page 116 and what are the questions that have been "assigned" by God?*

? *How does your answer to the question on page 116 relate to the things you see Christians in America focus on and spend their time on?*

? *How does the answer to the question on page 116 relate to the emphasis you place on the issues and concerns in your life?*

Chapter notes

While Paul was waiting for them in Athens, he was greatly distressed to see that the city was full of idols. So he reasoned in the synagogue with the Jews and the God-fearing Greeks, as well as in the marketplace day by day with those who happened to be there. A group of Epicurean and Stoic philosophers began to dispute with him. Some of them asked, "What is this babbler trying to say?" Others remarked, "He seems to be advocating foreign gods." They said this because Paul was preaching the good news about Jesus and the resurrection.

Acts 17:16–18

Praise be to the God and Father of our Lord Jesus Christ! In his great mercy he has given us new birth into a living hope through the resurrection of Jesus Christ from the dead, and into an inheritance that can never perish, spoil or fade—kept in heaven for you, who through faith are shielded by God's power until the coming of the salvation that is ready to be revealed in the last time.

1 Peter 1:3–5

Chapter 5
Application

Hopefully, as you worked your way through the preceding chapters, you thought about and discussed some things that are much larger than the story on which this discussion guide is based. Perhaps someone in the group said something that caused you to reevaluate an area of your life—maybe some priorities or the impact your life is having on those around you. Maybe the guide was a refresher course on Christ's resurrection. Maybe the reflection and discussion has even led you to pray about specific situations in your life.

But now what?

The following are summary questions that will hopefully help move the group's discussion and reflections from the theoretical to the practical, from platitudes to action.

Read Acts 17:16–34.

We stand in a place similar to that of Paul when he was in Athens. Athens was filled with false gods, hedonism, sin, brokenness, empty pride, idle chatter, misguided nationalism, and lost souls. So is America.

Describe our culture and how it might be similar to Athens as described in Acts 17.

But Paul made a choice. Rather than focus on the idolatry and brokenness of the culture that surrounded him, he decided to focus on the truth and the only answer to the Athenians' lost condition. He spoke about Jesus and His resurrection. He spoke about Jesus and His resurrection so much that some actually thought Paul was talking about two new gods (the god named Jesus and the god named Resurrection). Though the Athenians' misunderstanding might reflect some thick-headedness on their part, it certainly reveals that Paul's emphasis on the resurrection must have been quite strong in order for them to reach such a conclusion.

When people hear you talk about your faith, what do they think are your most important issues?

How we live our lives is, of course, vitally important to our ability to be effective witnesses to Christ and His resurrection. As you recall, Wil's mom and dad's witness (if you can call it that) actually drove Wil from Christ. Think hard and critically about this next question.

What does your life communicate to those around you? Would your life attract someone to Christ, drive someone away from Christ, or neither? Why?

Would your life convince someone that you believe Christ's resurrection is the most important event in history and that, because of it, you have hope beyond measure?

Some scholars debate the effectiveness of Paul's sermon in Athens (Acts 17: 22–31). A main criticism of his sermon is that it didn't cover the normal topics we expect to hear in an evangelistic sermon.

What makes something an effective presentation of the gospel?

Paul started where the people were (physically, intellectually, and spiritually) and led them to Christ and His resurrection. As to the success, we know there is rejoicing in heaven when one person is saved. According to Acts 17:34, "a few" believed. Since "a few" means more than one, we can conclude that Paul's faithfulness in proclaiming Christ and His resurrection led to a celebration in heaven. Paul's presentation was successful.

Since the situation we find ourselves in is so much like what Paul observed in Athens, shouldn't we consider following his example and spend our time focusing on Jesus and His resurrection rather than on all the less important issues that often consume our time and energy?

Is there something in your life you are so focused on that you are neglecting more important issues? What?

Take some time and pray about it.

Now, what are you going to do?

Nothing would please the author more than if Christians used *Wil's Bones* as an evangelistic tool to stimulate conversations with non-Christians about Jesus and His resurrection.

The ideal way to use this book (or any of his books) is to:

1) Read the book.

2) Consider whom you would like to talk with about the gospel but can't figure out where to start.

3) Pray for the Holy Spirit's guidance and that God will reveal Himself to that person.

4) Give or lend the person a copy of the book. Since most non-Christian stores and libraries call Kevin Bowen's books mysteries or thrillers (not Christian fiction), you can legitimately say it is a mystery or a thriller, which might make them more willing to read it.

5) Follow up and talk with the person about the book. There is plenty of non-threatening material in *Wil's Bones* to talk about. Ask questions such as:
- Kathreen is one wicked woman, isn't she?
- Did the politicians remind you of anyone?
- What did you think of Kenny Reno's monologue?
- Who is your favorite character?

In your conversation, you will not only learn about the person, you will probably have fun discussing the book. You will also demonstrate that Christians are more than just Bible-quoting automatons who are incapable of enjoying a good story.

6) Next, ask a question such as:
- Do you know anyone like Wil?
- It is amazing how much Wil's dad's hypocrisy affected Wil, isn't it?
- Did you understand why finding the bones of Jesus would be such a big deal to Christians?
- What do you think really happened to the bones?
- Why do you think that?

Do not preach. Do not be rude. Do not force the issue. Do not be a chicken, either. Always remember that it is the Lord who draws people to Himself, not a slick presentation or persuasive words.

7) With that in mind, move to questions such as:

- How would you answer the question Steve asked Wil on page 243?
- What happens if you are wrong in your beliefs?
- You do realize, don't you, that if you were to die today, your decision not to decide on the resurrection could be an eternal decision?
- Would you be willing to let me share with you more about Christ and how much God loves you?

The above questions are just suggestions. The idea of using *Wil's Bones* as an evangelistic tool with a non-believing friend or family member is a sincere request. You can also use any other gospel-presenting book. The point is that we act. God died for our friends and family members. It is important that we not wait until it is too late to share with them the good news of our resurrected Lord.

? *Can you use this book as a springboard for conversation with one of the following?*

- *A family member?*
- *A non-Christian friend, neighbor, or co-worker?*
- *Someone you are not reconciled to?*
- *Anyone?*

? *When are you going to do it?*

Chapter notes

A Note From the Author of *Wil's Bones*

There is a huge divide between Christian media (books, movies, music) and secular media. On one end of the spectrum is Christian entertainment, which often contains a good message but does not appeal to non-Christians because of its quality or content. On the other end of the spectrum is secular entertainment that is often filled with Christless worldviews, filth, and godless messages. Compounding the situation is that, often, neither side fairly portrays the other. Christian media frequently portray non-Christians as amoral, ignorant, or stubborn. Secular media routinely portray Christians as intolerant, violent, stupid and, of course, hypocritical.

I wanted to produce a piece of entertainment that contained a Christian message yet would bridge this gap between Christian and non-Christian entertainment. I was thrilled that most secular stores and reviewers called *Wil's Bones* a mystery or a thriller, while many Christians called it Christian fiction. I hope non-Christians who read *Wil's Bones* enjoy it and encounter the gospel. I hope Christians who read *Wil's Bones* enjoy it and then use the book as a tool to reach non-Christians with the gospel.

I also wrote *Wil's Bones* with the hope of reminding Christians of what truly matters. In a day when we are blessed beyond measure, the church in America is amazingly self-consumed. As our brothers and sisters around the world are dying because of their desire to see others come to Christ, we seem to be caught up in contentious divisions, church building projects, and material comforts.

I believe one of the reasons for this misdirected focus is our complacency. Since we are not faced with imminent persecution or death because of our faith, we have grown lackadaisical concerning more important, eternal matters. If we knew we could be killed the next time we went to worship or mentioned Jesus, we most likely would spend more time thinking about the hope that is in us because of Christ's resurrection.

My sincere desire is that this discussion guide and *Wil's Bones* have reminded you of the absolute centrality and historicity of our Lord's resurrection. I also hope that, somehow, we Christians can set aside our many secondary issues and once again find our hope and our foundation in the resurrection of Jesus.

Kevin Bowen
Author, *Wil's Bones*

Other Works
by Kevin Bowen

The Third Funeral

The thrilling sequel to *Wil's Bones*

(ISBN 1930892144, August 2003)

Wil and Hope Wilson return to Washington D.C. Wil is on a sabbatical from his work at the Institute of Palestinian Archaeological Research. Hope is working as a correspondent for *The New York Times*. When Hope witnesses the crash of Freedom Airways' flight 2652 into an oil refinery, she is catapulted into the media limelight.

On the same day that Wil and Hope attend the funeral for Scott Kingman, Wil's atheistic college roommate who was killed in the crash, they also attend the funeral for Rochelle Jackson, the 17-year-old Christian babysitter of their son, Steven.

Hope's subsequent investigation of the airline disaster collides with Freedom Airways' ruthless CEO. As Hope unravels a tapestry of cold-blooded deception, she unknowingly draws her family into a dangerous matrix of conspiracy, kidnapping, revenge, and murder.

Interwoven with the plot, the author addresses the inevitability of death and the need to be reconciled with God.

Wil's Bones was good. *The Third Funeral* is even better.

And introducing ...

Other Works

Kevin Bowen's Next Book

Faith

The exciting sequel to *Wil's Bones* and *The Third Funeral*
(ISBN 1930892160, August 2004)

After two men confess to faking miracles on Elijah Matheson's television show, investigative journalist Hope Wilson exonerates the scandal-ridden televangelist of this specific accusation of fraud. When the diamond-adorned Matheson announces that Hope has converted to Christianity, Hope's *New York Times* editor and the police begin to question her motives and objectivity.

Infuriated by their suspicions, Hope takes a hiatus from their recriminations and leaves for Israel to deal with some personal matters. In Jerusalem, Hope has a harrowing experience following a terrorist attack. In the aftermath, Hope befriends a Palestinian Christian who has experienced incredible hardships because of his commitment to Christ.

When Hope returns to the States she discovers a note from the two men who were involved in the miracles on Matheson's show. Unprepared for what lies ahead, Hope becomes entangled in a web of murder, international conspiracy, money laundering, and fundamental questions of faith.

Wil's Bones and *The Third Funeral* are also available in abridged audio format from Oasis Audio (www.oasisaudio.com):

Wil's Bones
ISBN 1589260570 (2 cassettes, retail $17.99)

The Third Funeral
ISBN 1589262255 (6 CDs, retail $27.99)
ISBN 1589262247 (4 cassettes, retail $24.99)

The following are available from Engage Publishing:

The Third Funeral Discussion Guide: A Tool For Christian Reading Groups
64-page, 8.5" x 5.5" paperback booklet
ISBN: 1930892152
(Sold in packs of 6, retail: $8.95/pack)

Wil's Bones Discussion Guide: A Tool For Christian Reading Groups
64-page, 8.5" x 5.5" paperback booklet
ISBN: 1930892136
(Sold in packs of 6, retail: $8.95/pack)

For more information on these or other products, and for special offers and discount pricing, please visit Engage Publishing's Web site: www.engagepublishing.com

ENGAGE
PUBLISHING